Editor
Kim Fields

Editorial Project Manager
Mara Ellen Guckian

Editor-in-Chief
Sharon Coan, M.S. Ed.

Illustrator
Renée Christine Yates

Cover Artist
Brenda DiAntonis

Art Coordinator
Kevin Barnes

Art Director
Cjae Froshay

Imaging
Ralph Olmedo, Jr.

Product Manager
Phil Garcia

Publishers
Rachelle Cracchiolo, M.S. Ed.
Mary Dupuy Smith, M.S. Ed.

Beginning & Ending Sounds

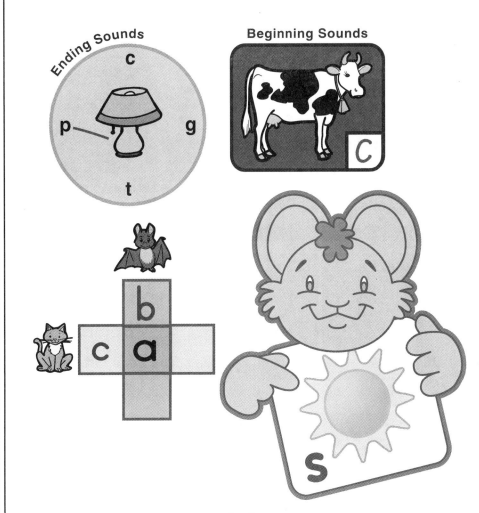

Author

Krista Pettit

Teacher Created Materials, Inc.
6421 Industry Way
Westminster, CA 92683
www.teachercreated.com

ISBN-0-7439-3391-5

©2003 Teacher Created Materials, Inc.
Made in U.S.A.

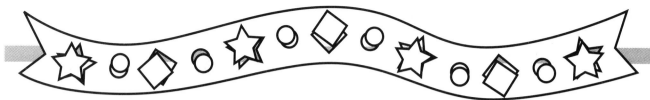

Table of Contents

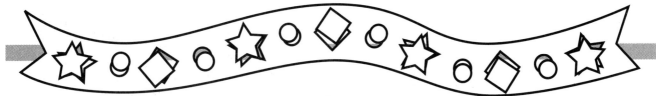

Introduction

Getting children ready for academic success should begin early. It is important, during these early years, to shape children's attitudes toward school and learning in a positive manner. Young children need frequent repetition and simplified directions. The activities should be engaging and visually stimulating. The purpose of this workbook series is to promote children's development and learning in an enjoyable way. Each activity book is designed to introduce young learners to new concepts and reinforce ones already learned. The skill pages are perfect for enrichment, classroom practice, tutoring, home schooling, or just for fun.

In *Beginning and Ending Sounds*, students will focus on the following concepts:

- **Beginning Sounds**—Children practice recognizing consonant sounds at the beginning of simple words. Using a combination of visual, aural, and tactile senses supports the development of phonemic awareness. When children see, hear, and touch the initial sound of a word, they become familiar with the concepts related to beginning sounds.

- **Ending Sounds**—By building on skills learned in the first section, children learn the more difficult task of discerning consonant sounds in word endings. To aid in this task, this book uses everyday words common to children's environments. These words activate the children's prior knowledge, enabling them to focus on the word itself (as opposed to the interpretation of the word).

- **Beginning and Ending Sounds**—Children review consonant sounds at the beginning and ending of a word using acquired skills. Children must synthesize prior knowledge to complete the complex task. This section provides opportunities for children to focus on the multistep process of identifying the beginning and ending sounds in the same word. The practice pages are designed to facilitate future literacy success.

Parents can use this workbook series to reinforce skills learned at home and/or school. Completing these skill pages together with their parents allows youngsters the opportunity to practice newly acquired knowledge in a stress-free environment. Because some of the activities require cutting and pasting, photocopying these pages is suggested. Copying activities onto cardstock or heavy paper makes it easier for beginning cutters to grasp and manipulate the paper.

This workbook series will enhance children's abilities to retain new skills. Because the pages can be utilized for seat work, homework, or home practice, the workbook pages are resources that can benefit children in a variety of environments. The skill pages feature easy-to-follow directions. This type of independent work gives children the support needed to internalize new concepts in an enjoyable and meaningful way.

Name_____

Flower Power

Directions: Cut out the flowers. Look at each picture and glue it above the pot with the corresponding *beginning* sound. Draw stems and leaves for the flowers.

Name_____

Pet Collar Partners

Directions: Cut out the letter boxes. Look at the letter on each one and glue it on the collar of the animal (cat, dog, rabbit, guinea pig) with the corresponding *beginning* sound.

Name_____

Little Bear's Baseball Game

Directions: Circle each object in the picture *beginning* with the /b/ sound. Color the circled objects.

Name_____

Writing in the Sand

Directions: Trace the *beginning* letter of each object. Color the objects.

Farmyard Letter Fun

Directions: Write the *beginning* sound for each animal in the corresponding box.

Name_____

Zoo Visit

Directions: Look at each animal and the letter above it. Circle each animal and letter pair with a matching *beginning* sound.

Name_____

School Matchup

 •

Directions: Look at the letters and pictures inside of them. Circle each picture with a corresponding *beginning* sound. Cross out each picture *beginning* with a different letter sound.

Name_____

Colorful Clowns

- Color each hat *beginning* with the /r/ sound red.

- Color each hat *beginning* with the /p/ sound purple.

- Color each hat *beginning* with the /y/ sound yellow.

- Color each hat *beginning* with the /g/ sound green.

 •

Directions: Look at the pictures in the hats. Color each hat following the coloring directions above.

Name_____

Pond Pals

Directions: Look at the pond animals. Circle each animal *beginning* with the /f/ sound. Draw a box around each animal *beginning* with the /r/ sound. Place an X over each animal *beginning* with the /s/ sound.

Name_____

Toy Match

Directions: Draw a line from each picture on the left to a picture with a matching *beginning* sound on the right.

Name_____

On a Roll

m s r

b k c

t d s

l f r

Directions: Circle the *beginning* sound for each picture.

Lunch Break

I   n   p   j   h   g

Directions: Cut out the letters. Look at each picture and glue the letter with the corresponding *beginning* sound in its box. Color the pictures.

Name_____

Kitchen Sounds

Directions: Look at each letter. Color the pictures in each row *beginning* with that sound.

Name_____

Ship Trip

Directions: Look at the scene. Color each object *beginning* with the /sh/ sound.

Name_____

Chicken Lunch

Directions: Cut out the pictures. Glue each one *beginning* with the /ch/ sound on the chicken.

18

Name_____

Digraph Match

ch	sh	th

Directions: Look at the pictures. Cut out each one and glue it under the column with the corresponding *beginning* sound.

#3391 Beginning & Ending Sounds

Let's Begin

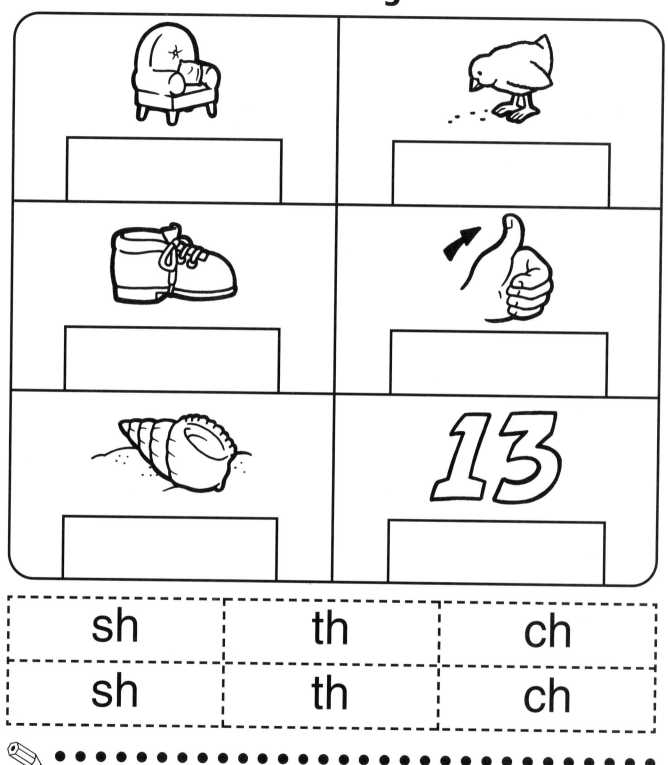

sh	th	ch
sh	th	ch

Directions: Cut out each digraph and glue it under a picture *beginning* with that sound. Color the pictures.

#3391 Beginning & Ending Sounds   20   © *Teacher Created Materials, Inc.*

Name_____

In My Bedroom

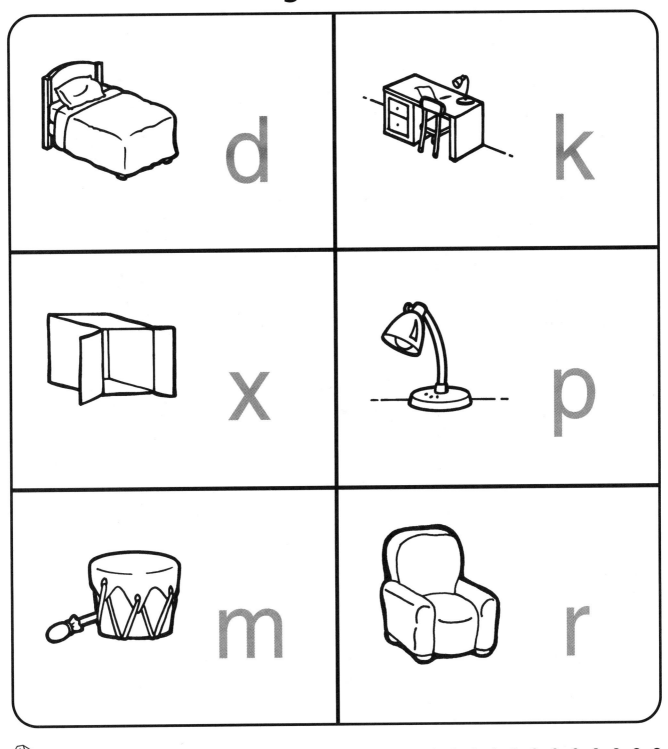

Directions: Trace the *ending* letter for each object. Color the pictures.

#3391 Beginning & Ending Sounds

Name_____

Puppy Love

- Draw a line from the puppy to each picture *ending* with the /n/ sound.

- Cross out each picture *ending* with the /t/ sound.

Directions: Follow the directions above. Color the puppy and something he might like to play with.

Name_____

Tool Time

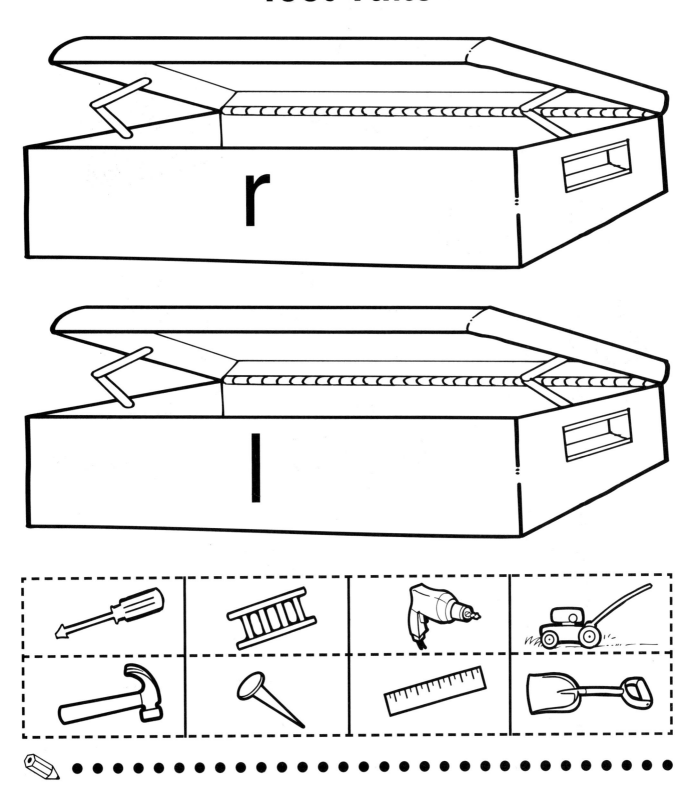

Directions: Look at the letters on the toolboxes. Cut out the tools and glue them into the box with the corresponding *ending* sound.

Line It Up

m

p   t

n

t

b   w

r

d

j   l

f

c

p   g

t

h

r   k

d

t

s   v

b

Directions: Look at the picture in the middle of each circle. Draw a line from the picture to its *ending* sound.

Name_____

Baby Endings

Directions: Look at the pictures. Write the *ending* sound for each baby item in the appropriate box. Color the pictures.

Name_____

Outfit Roundup

Directions: Look at the letters and the pictures inside of them. Circle each object with a corresponding *ending* sound. Cross out each picture with a different *ending* sound.

Name_____

Petal Pusher

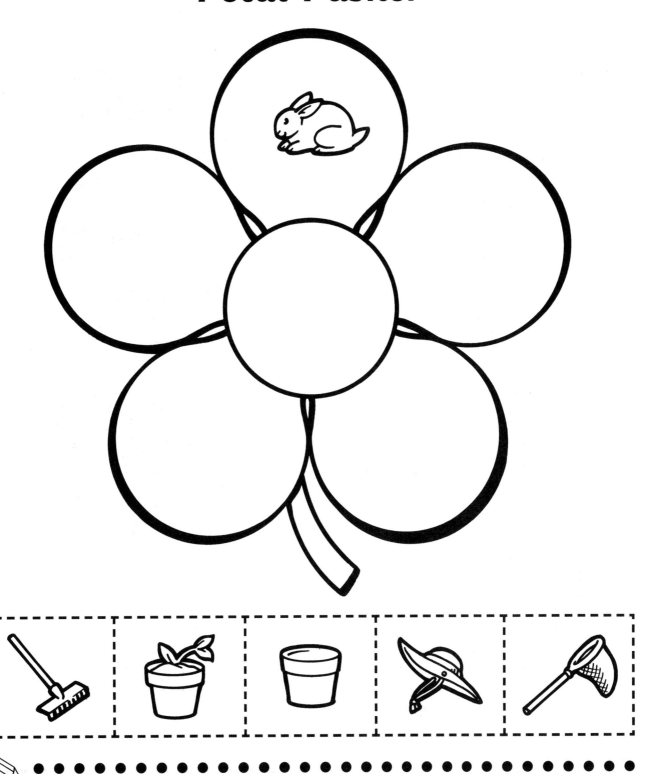

Directions: Cut out each picture *ending* with the /t/ sound and glue it on a petal. The first one has been done for you.

27

Name_____

Beach Towel Game

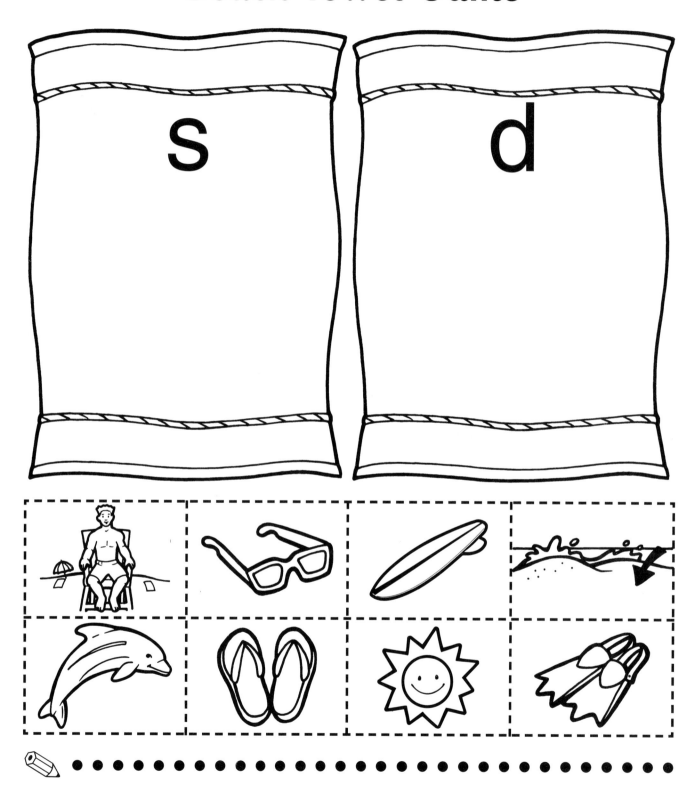

S

d

Directions: Look at the letters on the towels. Cut out the pictures. Glue each one on the towel with a corresponding *ending* sound. Some pictures will not be used.

Name_____

On the Farm

	k b n
	t g r
	n r t
	g s l
	k b m

 •

Directions: Look at the animals. Circle the correct *ending* letter that corresponds to each picture. Color the pictures.

Name_____

Let's Shop!

Directions: Look at the pictures. Color each food that has a corresponding *ending* sound.

#3391 Beginning & Ending Sounds   30   © *Teacher Created Materials, Inc.*

Name_____

T-Shirt Designs

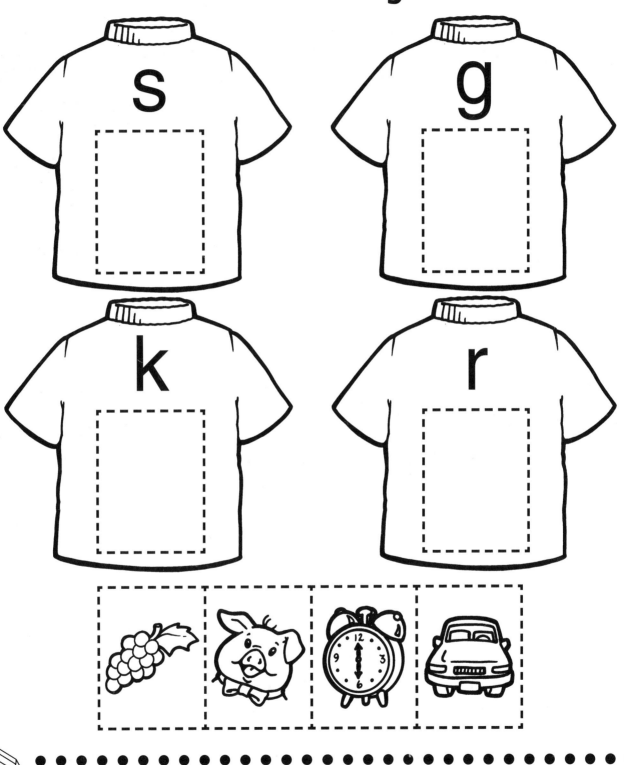

Directions: Cut out each design. Glue each design on the T-shirt with a corresponding *ending* sound.

Spectacular Sky

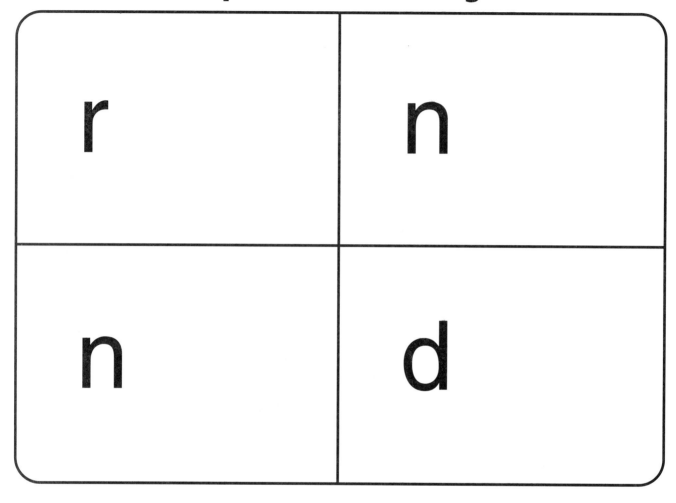

r	n
n	d

Directions: Cut out each picture and glue it beside the corresponding *ending* sound.

Name_____

Animal Roundup

n k p	c r t
f l g	k p n
s w d	b k t

✎ •

Directions: Look at the animals. Circle the corresponding *ending* sound for each picture. Color the animals.

Name_____

Ending Sound Matchup

Directions: Look at each letter. Circle the picture in each row with the corresponding *ending* sound.

Name_____

Happy Endings

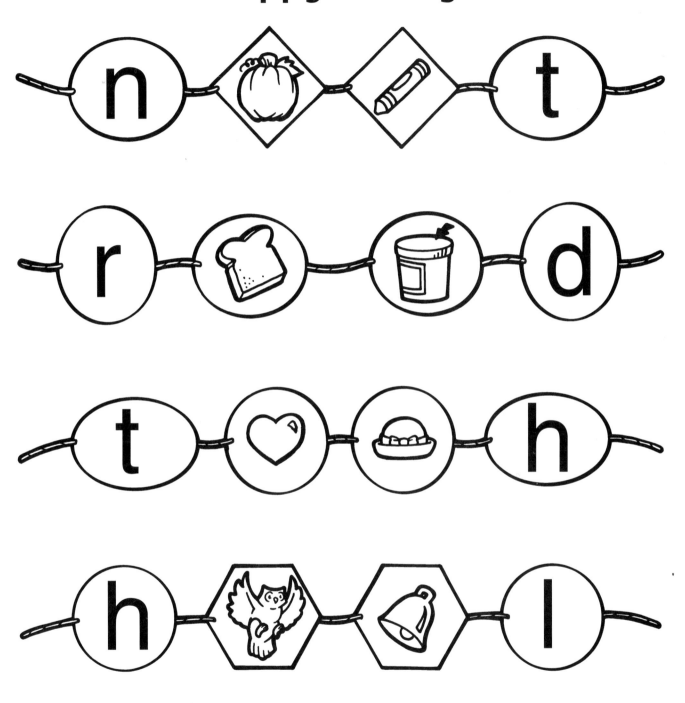

 ●

Directions: Look at the pictures on each necklace. Color the bead that has the same *ending* sound as the pictures.

Name_____

On the Move

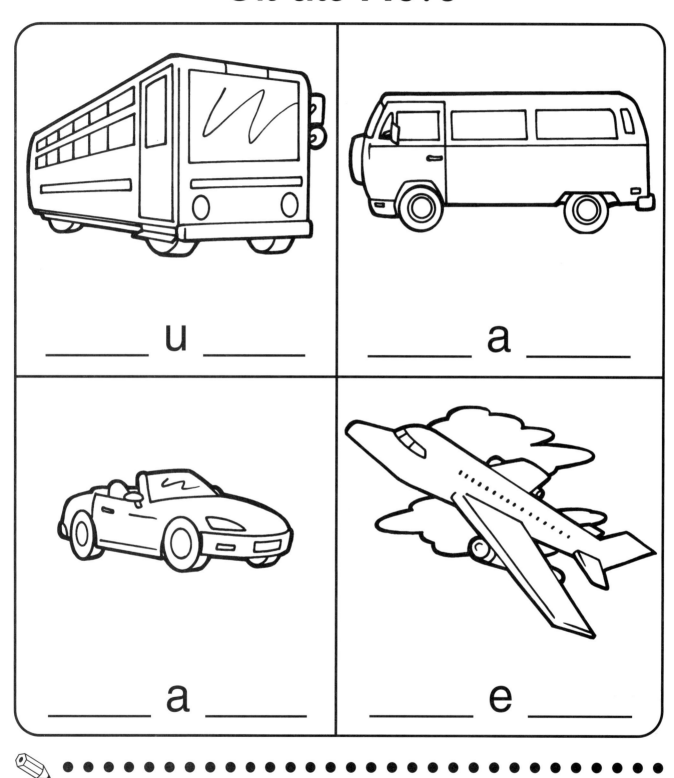

____ u ____

____ a ____

____ a ____

____ e ____

Directions: Write the *beginning* and *ending* letters for each picture. Color the pictures.

Name_____

Snowy Day

✎ •

Directions: Look at the pictures. Write the *beginning* and *ending* letters for each picture on the appropriate blanks.

Word Fun

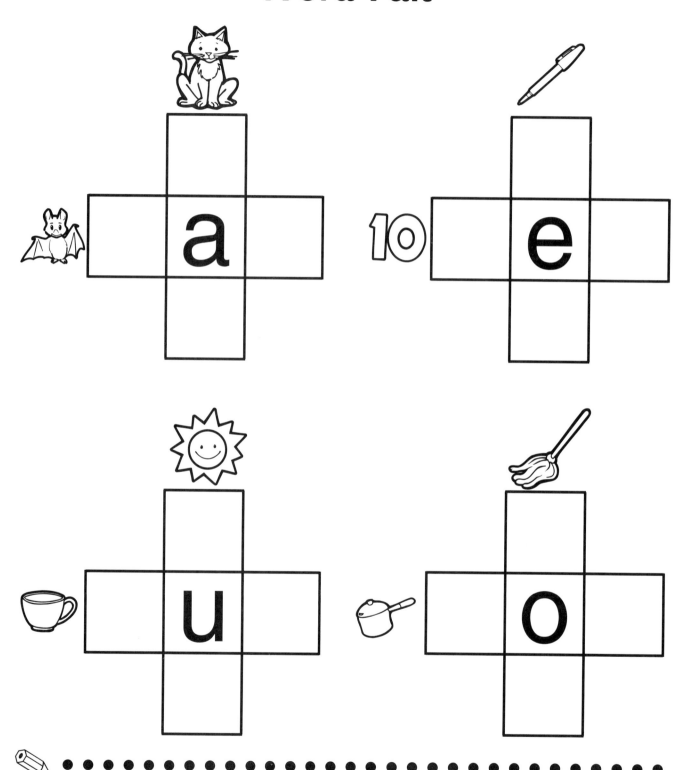

Directions: Complete each puzzles by filling in the missing *beginning* and *ending* sounds that correspond to the picture clues.

#3391 Beginning & Ending Sounds   38   © Teacher Created Materials, Inc.

Name_____

What Do You Hear?

Directions: Look at the objects. Draw a line from each object on the left to its corresponding *beginning* and *ending* sounds on the right.

Name_____

School Letter Fill-Ins

_____en

p   c   t

_____ape

f   t   m

_____ook

t   z   b

bal_____

b   l   m

des_____

g   k   n

bu_____

d   h   s

Directions: Look at the pictures. Circle the appropriate letter to complete each word. Fill in the blank with the correct letter.

Name_____

Word Match

bat

hen

cat

dog

pig

bug

Directions: Cut out the words. Glue each one in the box under its corresponding picture. A vowel hint is written under each animal.

Name_____

Sailing Away

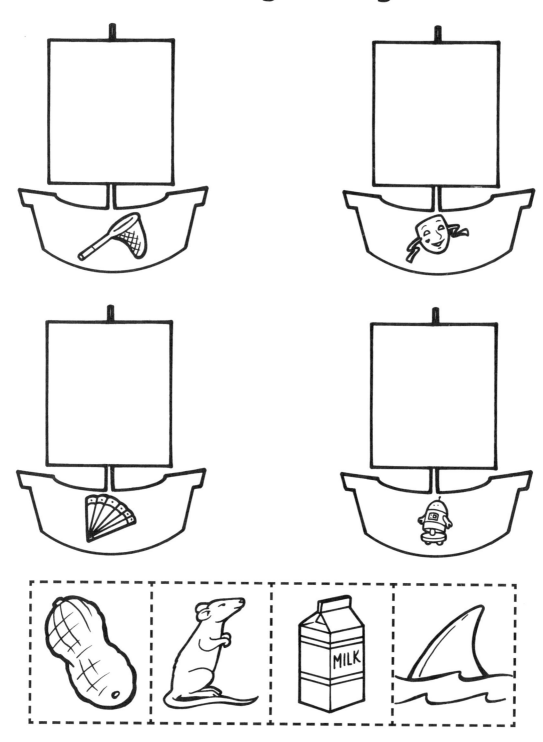

Directions: Cut out each picture. Glue each one above the boat with the picture having the corresponding *beginning* and *ending* sounds.

Name_____

Fishy Sounds

Directions: Look at the pictures. Draw a line from each fish to a fishing rod with corresponding *beginning* and *ending* sounds.

Name_____

Bubble Burst

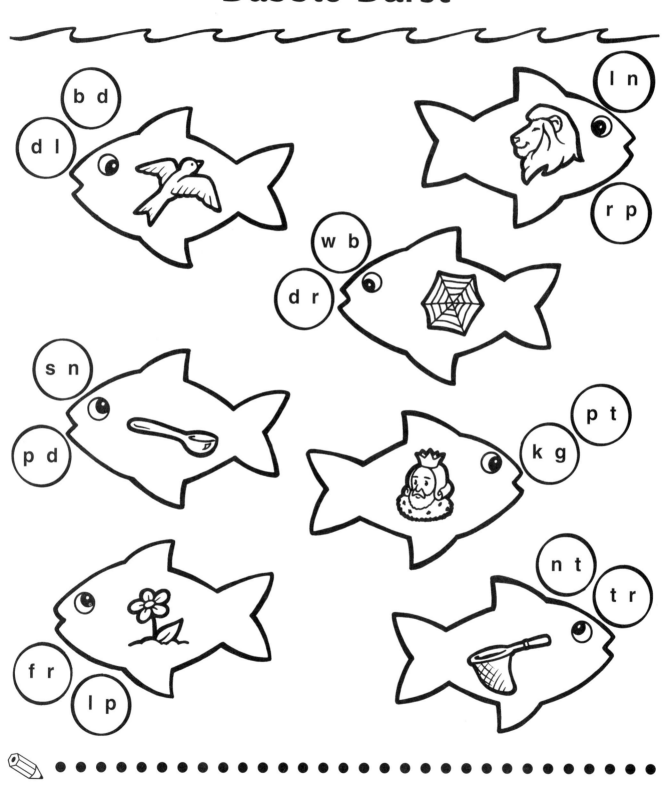

Directions: Look at the picture in each fish. Color the bubble with corresponding *beginning* and *ending* sounds.

Name_____

Spell a Word

a

u

a

e

e

| b | c | g | j | n |
| n | p | r | s | t |

Directions: Cut out the letters. Look at each picture. What is the *beginning* sound? What is the *ending* sound? Find the *beginning* and *ending* letters for each word and glue them in the appropriate spaces.

Name_____

Cut Ups

g s	b k

Directions: Cut out the pictures. Glue each one under the corresponding *beginning* and *ending* sounds.

Name_____

Start to Finish

© Teacher Created Materials, Inc.

Directions: Look at the letters. Circle the picture or pictures in each row with corresponding *beginning* and *ending* sounds.

 #3391 Beginning & Ending Sounds

Name_____

On the Right Track

Directions: Circle the appropriate *beginning* and *ending* letters for each animal.